Beyond Binary: Understanding Transgenderism & Gender Identity In The 21st Century

Beyond Binary: Understanding Transgenderism and Gender Identity in the 21st Century

Amanda Walker

Published by Amanda Walker, 2023.

While every precaution has been taken in the preparation of this book, the publisher assumes no responsibility for errors or omissions, or for damages resulting from the use of the information contained herein.

BEYOND BINARY: UNDERSTANDING TRANSGENDERISM AND GENDER IDENTITY IN THE 21ST CENTURY

First edition. May 9, 2023.

ISBN: 979-8223199083

Written by Amanda Walker.

Contents

1. The debate of the century (intro)

2. Defining a woman throughout history

3. The Struggle of Transgender Woman

4. Biological Essentialism

5. Gender Dysphoria

6.Transgenderism in the Animal Kingdom

7.Transgender In Ancient Culture

8.Can Some Transgenderism be considered a Social Endemic?

9. What makes a man a man?

10. Biological Advantages and Concerns

What is a woman, and whether or not a man can really become a woman, (or a woman really become a man) is one of the great debates of the 21st century. As time presses on, more and more people – particularly youth, are identifying as Transgender or Non-binary and wanting equality. However many have raised concerns over how far that equality should go. Should transgender females (who are biological males and still bearing a penis) be allowed to use female spaces such as bathrooms? Should they be allowed to compete in woman sports if they have biological advantages that cannot be changed through surgery? If society allows transgender woman to fully enter and have true equality in female spaces, do we risk eradicating the protections and equality that females fought for the right to over the last 200+ years?

Defining a woman throughout history

The concept of womanhood has evolved over time and differs across cultures and societies. From ancient times to modern day, women have played various roles in society and have been defined in different ways. Understanding the historical and cultural definitions of womanhood is essential to understanding the ongoing struggle for gender equality and women's rights in modern society.

Ancient Definitions of Womanhood In ancient societies such as Mesopotamia, Egypt, Greece, and Rome, womanhood was defined primarily in terms of a woman's relationship to men. Women were expected to be wives and mothers, and their roles in society were largely limited to the domestic sphere. In ancient Greece, for example, women were not allowed to participate in politics or education, and their primary role was to bear children and manage the household. Similarly, in ancient Rome, women were expected to be loyal wives and mothers, and their legal status was dependent on their relationship to men. Women in these societies had limited autonomy and agency, and were often subject to the authority of their husbands or fathers.

Medieval and Renaissance Views of Womanhood During the Middle Ages and Renaissance, womanhood was viewed through the lens of Christianity, which had a significant impact on the role and status of women in society. Women were often viewed as inferior to men and were expected to be submissive and obedient to their husbands. However, there were some new roles that emerged for women during this time period. For example, women were able to become nuns and participate in religious life, which allowed them to have some autonomy and agency. Additionally, women such as

Hildegard von Bingen and Christine de Pizan were able to carve out spaces for themselves as scholars and writers.

The Enlightenment was a philosophical movement that emerged in Europe in the 18th century (1715-1789) It was characterized by a focus on reason, rationality, and scientific inquiry, and a rejection of traditional authority and dogma. The Enlightenment thinkers believed in the power of reason and education to bring about progress and social change, and they sought to apply scientific methods to understand and improve human society.

During the Enlightenment there were significant advances in science, philosophy, and politics. Thinkers such as John Locke, Voltaire, Jean-Jacques Rousseau, and Immanuel Kant developed new ideas about individual rights, democracy, and the role of government. These ideas had a profound impact on the Western world, shaping the development of modern democracy, human rights, and social justice movements.

In addition to its political and philosophical ideas, the Enlightenment also had a significant impact on culture and art. The movement was characterized by a focus on reason and naturalism, and a rejection of the ornate and extravagant art and architecture of previous eras. This led to the development of new artistic styles such as Neoclassicism, which emphasized simplicity, clarity, and rationality.

Overall, the Enlightenment was a pivotal moment in European history, characterized by a rejection of traditional authority and a focus on reason, science, and progress. Its ideas and values have had a lasting impact on modern Western society, shaping our understanding of politics, philosophy, science, and culture.

There was also the emergence of feminism during the Enlightenment, ideas about reason and equality began to challenge traditional views of women's role in society. Feminist thinkers such as Mary Wollstonecraft argued for women's rights and autonomy, and advocated for education and equal opportunities for women.

Mary Wollstonecraft (1759-1797) was an English writer and philosopher who is considered to be one of the founding figures of modern feminism. She wrote extensively on women's rights, education, and social and political equality.

In 1792, Wollstonecraft published her most famous work, "A Vindication of the Rights of Woman," in which she argued that women were not inherently inferior to men, but were instead held back by their lack of education and social and legal restrictions. She believed that women should have access to the same educational opportunities as men, and that women's rights were essential to the progress of society as a whole.

Wollstonecraft's ideas were groundbreaking at the time and sparked heated debates about the role of women in society. Her work was influential in the development of modern feminist thought and continues to be studied and discussed today.

However, these early feminist movements were limited in their scope and did not address the experiences of women of color or working-class women. Additionally, women's legal rights and status were still limited in many parts of the world.

In the 1960s and 1970s, second-wave feminism emerged, which focused on issues such as reproductive rights, workplace discrimination, and sexual violence. This movement was more inclusive than previous feminist movements, and addressed the intersectional experiences of women of color and working-class women. Since then, feminist movements have continued to evolve and expand, with the inclusion of transgender and queer women, and a focus on issues such as gender-based violence, pay equity, and representation in politics and media.

In the 1980s, feminist movements began to expand to include transgender women, who were often excluded from mainstream feminist discourse. This shift was driven in part by the emergence of the transgender rights movement, which sought to challenge the discrimination and marginalization faced by transgender individuals. Transgender women began to participate in feminist organizing and advocacy, and their experiences of oppression and marginalization became an important part of the feminist discourse.

Transgender women have been involved in feminist movements for decades, although their participation has often been controversial and subject to debate within the feminist community.

One notable example of a transgender woman who was involved in feminist activism is Sylvia Rivera (1951-2002). Rivera was a Latina transgender activist who was a key figure in the Stonewall riots of 1969, which are often credited with launching the modern LGBTQ rights movement. She was also a founding member of the Gay Liberation Front and the Gay Activists Alliance, and advocated for the rights of LGBTQ people, people of color, and other marginalized groups throughout her life.

Another example is Marsha P. Johnson (1945-1992), a Black transgender activist who was also involved in the Stonewall riots and was a prominent figure in the LGBTQ rights movement in the 1970s and 1980s. She co-founded the Street Transvestite Action Revolutionaries (STAR), an organization that provided housing and support to transgender and gender nonconforming youth in New York City.

However, it is worth noting that not all transgender women identify as feminists, and some feminist movements have historically been exclusionary towards transgender women. The relationship between transgender women and feminism is complex and continues to be a topic of debate and discussion within the feminist community.

One of the key challenges facing transgender women in feminist spaces was the notion of "biological essentialism," which held that a person's sex determined their gender identity and social role. This idea was at odds with the experiences of many transgender individuals, who felt that their gender identity did not align with their assigned sex at birth. Feminist thinkers and activists began to challenge the notion of biological essentialism, arguing that gender was a social construct rather than a biological fact.

Transgender women also brought attention to issues such as access to healthcare, employment discrimination, and violence against transgender individuals, which had often been overlooked by mainstream feminist movements. Feminist activists began to work alongside transgender individuals to advocate for policies and laws that would protect transgender rights and address the unique challenges faced by transgender women.

Overall, the inclusion of transgender women in feminist movements in the 1980s marked an important shift in the feminist discourse, broadening the focus from gender as a binary concept to a more nuanced understanding of gender identity and expression. While there is still much work to be done to achieve full equality for transgender individuals, the contributions of transgender women to feminist movements have helped to make the fight for gender equality more inclusive and intersectional.#

The struggles of a Transgender Woman

Transgender women face unique challenges and obstacles in their lives, from navigating legal and social barriers to accessing healthcare and employment,to dealing with discrimination and violence. Much in the way cisgendered woman have through out history. Understanding these experiences is crucial to advocating for the rights of transgender women and creating a more inclusive and equitable society.

Legal Barriers:

One of the major legal barriers facing transgender women is the lack of legal recognition of their gender identity. In many countries, transgender individuals are required to undergo gender-affirming surgeries or meet other strict requirements in order to legally change their gender. This can be a costly and time-consuming process, and many transgender individuals cannot meet these requirements, leaving them unable to obtain legal recognition of their gender identity. This can have serious consequences, such as being denied access to healthcare, housing, and employment.

Another legal barrier facing transgender women is discrimination in the criminal justice system. Transgender women are more likely to be profiled, arrested, and incarcerated than cisgender women, and they are often subjected to violence and abuse while in custody. In some countries, transgender women are even placed in male prisons, putting them at risk of physical and sexual assault.

Social Barriers:

Transgender women also face a range of social barriers, from discrimination and stigma to limited access to healthcare and support services. Transgender women are often the targets of harassment and violence, both in public spaces and online, and they may face rejection from family and friends.

Access to healthcare is another major concern for transgender women, who often face barriers to accessing gender-affirming healthcare such as hormone therapy and gender reassignment surgery. In many cases, healthcare providers may lack knowledge and training in transgender healthcare, or may hold biases and stereotypes about transgender individuals.

Examples of Struggles and Barriers:

In the United States, transgender women of color face particularly severe challenges, including higher rates of violence and discrimination. The Human Rights Campaign reports that transgender women of color are disproportionately likely to experience violence and murder, with at least 26 transgender people killed in 2019, the vast majority of whom were transgender women of color.

In other countries, such as Russia and Malaysia, transgender individuals face legal and social barriers that restrict their access to healthcare, employment, and other basic rights. In Russia, for example, a law banning "propaganda of non-traditional sexual relations" has been used to justify discrimination against transgender individuals and other members of the LGBTQ+ community.

Conclusion:

Overall, transgender women face significant legal and social barriers that limit their ability to live full and equal lives. These barriers, which include lack of legal recognition of their gender identity, discrimination in the criminal justice system, violence and harassment, and limited access to healthcare and support services, underscore the urgent need for greater awareness and advocacy on behalf of transgender individuals. By working to dismantle these barriers and create a more inclusive and equitable society, we can ensure that transgender women and other members of the LGBTQ+ community are able to live free from discrimination and violence.

The rise of feminism and the desire for the transgender community to have equality exposed that both groups had a lot of the same (or very similar) desires, needs and demands. By working together, they increased their numbers to get their voices heard. It is here that females and trans-females worked together to become 'women'. To become something more than were our fairer sex are more than child bearing cattle.

Biological Essentialism

Biological essentialism is the belief that certain biological characteristics, such as sex and gender, determine fundamental aspects of an individual's identity and behavior. This idea has been used to argue that men and women are inherently different and suited to different roles in society, and that gender inequality is a natural and inevitable outcome of biological differences.

Proponents of biological essentialism argue that it is grounded in scientific fact, and that acknowledging biological differences between men and women can help to explain differences in behavior and performance in areas such as sports, math, and science. They also argue that biological essentialism can provide a justification for gender-based policies and practices, such as single-sex education or gender-based affirmative action.

Critics of biological essentialism, on the other hand, argue that it is a flawed and outdated concept that reinforces gender stereotypes and discrimination. They point out that biological differences between men and women are often overstated or misunderstood, and that social and cultural factors play a much larger role in shaping individual behavior and identity. They argue that by focusing on biological essentialism, we risk overlooking the real social and cultural factors that contribute to gender inequality and discrimination.

Moreover, they argue that biological essentialism is often used to justify harmful practices such as discrimination against transgender individuals or women in male-dominated fields. By asserting that biological characteristics determine individual behavior and identity, biological essentialism can limit individuals' ability to express themselves and pursue their interests free from gender-based stereotypes and discrimination.

There are several biological differences between men and women other than genitalia, including:

1. Chromosomes: Men typically have one X and one Y chromosome, while women have two X chromosomes. Some individuals may have three sex chromosomes (XXX, XXY, XYY), which can result in differences in physical and/or cognitive development. However, it is important to note that the presence of additional sex chromosomes does not necessarily determine a person's gender identity or sexual orientation.

2. Hormones: Men produce more testosterone, while women produce more estrogen and progesterone. Testosterone will aid in and increase in muscle mass, bone density and an increase in mood and well being. Estrogen promotes better cognitive and memory function, lower choloesterol levels and promotes bone health

3. Body composition: Men generally have more muscle mass and less body fat, while women have more body fat and less muscle mass. Men also tend to have larger lung capacities. The larger lung capacity and muscle mass gives males an athletic advantage.

4. Reproductive system: Women have a uterus and are capable of carrying a pregnancy, while men do not have a uterus and cannot carry a pregnancy.

5. Bone density: Women generally have lower bone density than men, making them more susceptible to osteoporosis.

6. Metabolism: Men typically have a faster metabolism than women, allowing them to burn calories more quickly.

7. Brain structure: Studies have shown that men and women have differences in brain structure and function, particularly in areas related to language and spatial reasoning.studies have shown that there are some differences in brain structure and function between men and women, these differences are generally small and there is a significant overlap between the sexes. However, there are Some studies suggest that female brains may have advantages in certain areas, such as verbal communication, social cognition, and multitasking. For example, a study published in the journal "Brain and Language" found that women use more language areas of the brain than men, and another study published in "Psychological Science" found that women are better at reading emotional cues from facial expressions. Additionally, research has suggested that the female brain may have a larger corpus callosum, the bundle of fibers that connects the two hemispheres of the brain, which may enhance communication between the two sides of the brain. However, it is important to note that there is significant variation between individuals, and any differences between male and female brains should not be taken as absolute or determinative.

One study, for example, found that women tend to have better verbal memory and cognitive flexibility than men. Another study found that women's brains are better able to handle multiple tasks simultaneously, known as "multi-tasking." There is also some evidence to suggest that women may be better at processing emotional information and picking up on social cues.

It's important to note that while there are biological differences between men and women, there is also a wide range of individual variation within each gender, and gender identity is not determined solely by biology.

In summary, biological essentialism is a complex concept with important implications for gender equality and social justice. While some argue that acknowledging biological differences between men and women is necessary for understanding and addressing gender inequality, others argue that it reinforces harmful stereotypes and discrimination. The debate over biological essentialism is likely to continue, as we strive to create a more equitable and inclusive society for all.

Gender Dysphoria

Gender dysphoria is a medical condition in which an individual experiences significant distress or discomfort as a result of a mismatch between their gender identity and the sex assigned to them at birth. This distress can manifest in a variety of ways, including feeling like one's body does not match their gender identity, feeling uncomfortable or distressed in social situations where one's gender is misidentified or misunderstood, and experiencing significant psychological distress as a result of the incongruence between one's gender identity and biological sex.

Gender dysphoria is not the same as being gay, lesbian, or bisexual. It is also important to note that not all individuals who identify as transgender experience gender dysphoria. However, for those who do, the experience can be highly distressing and may significantly impact their mental health and overall quality of life. It is the lack of gender dysphoria that confuses onlookers as to whether or not someone is truly transgendered.

Gender dysphoria is recognized as a legitimate medical condition by many medical and psychiatric organizations, including the World Health Organization (WHO) and the American Psychological Association (APA). Treatment for gender dysphoria may involve a combination of medical interventions such as hormone therapy and surgery, as well as psychotherapy and social support. The goal of treatment is typically to alleviate the distress associated with gender dysphoria and help individuals live as their true selves. It is important to approach individuals with gender dysphoria with empathy, respect, and a commitment to providing them with the support and care they need to live fulfilling lives.

Gender dysphoria is a medical diagnosis that describes the distress or discomfort that some individuals may feel as a result of a mismatch between their gender identity and the sex assigned to them at birth. However, not all individuals who identify as transgender experience distress or discomfort related to their gender identity.

For some individuals, their gender identity is simply a core part of who they are, and they do not experience significant distress as a result of their gender identity. These individuals may still choose to transition to living as their true selves through medical interventions such as hormone therapy and surgery, but they may not meet the diagnostic criteria for gender dysphoria.

It is also important to note that the experience of being transgender is unique to each individual, and there is no one "right" way to be transgender. Some individuals may experience gender dysphoria, while others may not. The important thing is to support individuals in living as their true selves, whatever that may look like for them, and to provide them with the resources and care they need to thrive.

Diagnosing Gender Dysphoria

Gender dysphoria is typically diagnosed by a mental health professional, such as a psychologist or psychiatrist, through a process of clinical evaluation and assessment. The process may involve several steps, including a thorough evaluation of the individual's psychological and medical history, a discussion of their gender identity and experiences related to gender, and the administration of standardized diagnostic tests, such as the Diagnostic and Statistical Manual of Mental Disorders (DSM-5) criteria.

The DSM-5 criteria for gender dysphoria include several diagnostic criteria that must be met for a diagnosis to be made. These criteria include a marked incongruence between an individual's experienced/expressed gender and their assigned gender, a strong desire to be treated as the opposite gender, and significant distress or impairment in social, occupational, or other areas of functioning as a result of the incongruence between gender identity and assigned gender.

In addition to the DSM-5 criteria, a mental health professional may also use other diagnostic tools and assessments, such as clinical interviews and self-report measures, to help determine whether an individual is experiencing gender dysphoria.

It is important to note that the process of diagnosing gender dysphoria should be conducted in a supportive and affirming manner, and the individual's gender identity should be respected throughout the diagnostic process. A diagnosis of gender dysphoria is not a requirement for an individual to access medical interventions such as hormone therapy or surgery, and healthcare providers should work with individuals to determine the best course of treatment for their unique needs and circumstances.

Transgenderism in the Animal Kingdom

Being able to discuss our thoughts and feelings is a benefit that we have as humans over the rest of the animal kingdom. We can have conversations with humans and be diagnosed with a condition.

We still have little understanding what makes a person identifying as transgender. Whether is is all in the psyche, if it is due to society and the environment or if there are biological and genetic markers involved. Once upon a time homosexuality was a taboo abnormal human invention. It was in 1864 that a German scientist Karl Heinrich Ulrichs observed homosexual behaviour in Seagulls, but it wasn't until the 1980's when biologist Bruce Bagemihl published a book called "Biological Exuberance: Animal Homosexuality and Natural Diversity", which provided an extensive survey of same-sex behavior in over 450 animal species. This book helped to shift the understanding of homosexuality in animals from being considered unnatural or abnormal to being seen as a natural part of animal behavior. Since then, many other studies have provided evidence of same-sex behavior in animals, and it is now widely accepted that homosexuality is a natural and common occurrence in the animal kingdom. Mammals such as Dolphins, Male Lions, Giraffes and Sheep all display homosexual behaviour

So can we observe forms of Transgenderism or Gender fluidity in different species ?

There are several species of frogs that are known to change their sex in response to environmental cues such as the absence of mates or the presence of too many males. This is known as sex reversal or sex change. In some species, such as the African reed frog Hyperolius viridiflavus, individuals will change sex repeatedly throughout their lives in response to changing environmental conditions. In other species, such as the common reed frog Hyperolius marmoratus, females may change into males under certain conditions. This is thought to be an adaptation that helps maintain a balanced sex ratio in populations. However, frogs do not have XY or XX sex chromosomes like humans and other mammals. Instead, many species of frogs have a system of genetic sex determination known as the ZW system. In this system, females have two different sex chromosomes, ZW, while males have two of the same sex chromosomes, ZZ. The difference with these chromosomes is that unlike humans, they react to temperature and the lack of (or abundance of) hormones in an environment.

Some fish species, such as blue head wrasses, can change their gender throughout their lives in response to changes in the social and environmental context. Similarly, certain species of reptiles, such as the central bearded dragon, have been observed to change their sex from male to female or vice versa. But again, fish and reptiles carry different chromosomes to mammals

If we look at mammals, and in particularly primates there are several examples of primates that exhibit behaviours that could be considered "transgender" or "gender non-conforming" in order to gain social status.

One example is the female Japanese macaque, who will sometimes present her genitalia to another female in a behavior called "presenting." This behavior is typically associated with sexual receptivity in female primates, but in this context, it is used as a way for the presenting female to gain social status within her group.

Another example is the male gelada baboon, who will sometimes present his swollen, brightly coloured buttocks to other males in a behavior called "lip flipping." This behavior is usually seen in females during their estrus cycle, but the male gelada baboon uses it to signal dominance over other males and gain social status within his group.

There are also several examples of primates that exhibit male-like behavior to gain social status or dominance in their group, including:

1. Female baboons: Female baboons have been observed to engage in masculine behaviours such as fighting, displaying dominance, and even mounting other females in order to establish social rank within their group.

2. Female lemurs: In some lemur species, females will develop male-like genitalia and behavior in order to establish social dominance and increase their chances of mating with high-ranking males.

3. Female macaques: Female macaques have also been observed to display male-like behaviours, including mounting other females and exhibiting aggressive behavior in order to gain social status within their group.

Other animals that may behave as the opposite sex include
- Cuttlefish: Male cuttlefish sometimes display a female-like appearance and behavior to avoid detection by larger, aggressive males. This allows them to mate with females without being noticed.

– Bluegill sunfish: In populations where there is a shortage of males, some female bluegill sunfish will change their appearance and behavior to resemble males. This allows them to mate with females and gain access to the best breeding sites.

– -Spotted hyenas: Female spotted hyenas are larger and more dominant than males. They also have a pseudo-penis that is larger than the male's penis. This allows them to assert dominance over males and other females in their social group.

-Birds: In some bird species, females will display male-like plumage and behavior to attract mates or defend their territory.

-Red deer: In some populations of red deer, females will grow antlers like males, which allows them to compete for food and mates more effectively.

It's important to note that these behaviours are not necessarily indicative of transgender identities or gender dysphoria in these animals, but rather adaptive strategies for social success within their respective species. However, that being said, it could raise the question that if someone does not need to have Gender Dysphoria to be considered as trans, then like the these examples from the animal kingdom , is there some sort of social status to be gained by identifying as transgender in the 21st century? Is there a benefit to be gained, even if it is not an obvious one?

It also raises the question that if gender is a social construct constructed by humans and should be considered independent of biological sex then why are gender roles displayed in the animal kingdom?

What about Intersex People

One of the main arguments that the trans community will use to defend that biology is a factor to transgenderism rather than a psychological phenomenon is 'Intersex People'

Intersex conditions can manifest in a variety of ways and can involve chromosomal, hormonal, or anatomical differences that are not typical of male or female bodies. Some examples of intersex characteristics include:

1. Ambiguous genitalia: This is when the external genitals don't clearly appear as either male or female. It can range from genitalia that looks mostly male or mostly female to genitalia that is completely indeterminate.
2. Chromosomal differences: Most people are born with either XX or XY chromosomes, but some intersex people have other variations, such as XXY, XO, or XYY.
3. Hormonal differences: Intersex people may have variations in hormone levels, such as higher or lower levels of testosterone, oestrogen, or other hormones.
4. Reproductive system differences: Intersex people may have reproductive systems that are not typically male or female, such as undescended testes, ovaries that produce sperm, or a combination of male and female internal reproductive structures.
5. Other physical differences: Intersex people may have other physical differences that are not typical of male or female bodies, such as a combination of male and female secondary sex characteristics (such as breast development and facial hair), or differences in muscle mass, bone

density, or other physical traits.

Some intersex variations are apparent at birth, while others may not be discovered until later in life, such as during puberty. There are some cases where Intersex people have been assigned a gender at birth, only to discover that they are in fact the other sex when they arrive at puberty. This isn't an argument for Transgenderism being biological, rather then mistakes and guess work being done at birth as it is too hard to tell.

Intersex variations can cause medical complications depending on the specific variation. Some intersex variations may require medical intervention, such as surgery or hormone therapy, to address health issues or for cosmetic reasons. Others may not require medical intervention at all. It's important to note that not all intersex people will experience medical complications, and each individual's experience is unique.

The reason that the use of intersex people is a poor argument for transgenderism being biological is that, Intersex people are genetic anomalies. We know through centuries of research how the human body works. Some intersex people NEED medical care in order to maintain a biological norm, whereas a biologically, there is nothing wrong with a transgender person.

In mammals, some studies have suggested that the prevalence of intersex conditions (where an individual has ambiguous genitalia or reproductive organs which are an anomaly) may be higher in some species than previously thought, which could indicate that transgenderism could be more common in these species as well. However, more research is needed to better understand the prevalence and nature of transgenderism in different animal species.

Transgenderism in Ancient Culture

The concept of transgender identity as it is understood today is a relatively recent development, and it can be challenging to apply modern labels and understandings to historical and cultural examples. However, there are examples of gender nonconformity and non-binary gender identities in various ancient cultures around the world.

For example, in many Indigenous cultures in North America, two-spirit people held a revered and respected place in society. They were often seen as having both masculine and feminine traits, and were believed to possess unique spiritual gifts. In some cases, two-spirit individuals were considered to be outside the traditional gender binary and held important roles in their communities, such as healers, artists, and leaders.

In ancient India, the Hijra community is believed to have existed for thousands of years. Hijra individuals are assigned male at birth but may identify as female or non-binary, and they are often seen as a third gender in Indian culture. While they have historically faced stigma and discrimination, they have also been celebrated for their unique skills and contributions to society.

There are also examples of gender-nonconforming individuals in ancient Greece and Rome, such as the philosopher and teacher Epictetus, who was said to have been born with a physical disability and referred to himself as a eunuch. In some cases, individuals who identified outside of the traditional gender binary were celebrated for their unique qualities and contributions to society.

Elagabalus, a Roman emperor who reigned from 218 to 222 AD. Elagabalus was assigned male at birth but preferred to present as female and was known to wear women's clothing, make-up, and wigs. They also married several women and were rumoured to have had male lovers.

Another example is the 18th-century French writer and diplomat Chevalier d'Eon, who was assigned male at birth but lived as a woman for much of their life. D'Eon dressed as a woman and was referred to with female pronouns, and even fought in the Seven Years' War as a female spy.

The 81 Genders

The number of ways to describe gender can be confusing, as there are at least 81 different cultural terms to describe gender constructs (and that number is growing). This doesn't mean that there are 81 different genders, but rather that there are 81 different ways in which gender is conceptualized and expressed across various cultures. It is worth noting that different cultures assign different attribute to genders. The following list provides a collection of terms used to refer to different gender identifications, but it is not an exhaustive list. There may be many more terms from different cultures around the world that are not included.

1. Acault (Myanmar)

Acault is a gender from Buddhist people of Myanmar. It describes people who are AMAB (assigned male at birth) who have been possessed by a female spirit god named Manguedon who has imparted femininity on them. Acaults are often seen as wise shamans and seers

2. AFAB

AFAB stand for 'assigned female at birth'. It is a gender identity often assigned to people if there is for any reason a need to know a person's birth gender, especially if that person no longer associates with that gender. It acknowledges that birth genders are assigned through cultural inscription.

3. Agender

Agendered people do not have a gender. They are considered genderless or genderfree and do not fit on a masculine-feminine spectrum.

4. Aliagender

Aliagendered people are neither male, female, or agendered. They are people who experience a gender identity that does not fit on the masculine-feminine spectrum but nonetheless feel a gendered identity.

5. Alyha and Hwame (Mohave)

The Mohave people of the south-western United States have two non-cis genders, alyha and hwame. Alyha are male-assigned people who dress and behave like women. Hwame are female-assigned people who dress and behave like men. Both alyha and hwame take on traditionally non-gendered roles. They are also both seen as having special spiritual powers.

6. AMAB

AMAB stands for 'assigned male at birth'. Like AFAB, it is a gender identity often assigned to people if there is for any reason a need to know a person's birth gender, especially if that person no longer associates with that gender. It acknowledges that birth genders are assigned through cultural inscription.

7. Androgynous

An androgynous person is neither male or female. Their identity is considered ambiguous. Often, androgynes express elements of both masculine and feminine identities at different times.

8. Aporagender

Aporagender people are those who do not identify with any specific gender. They may feel that they have no gender, or that their gender is undefined. This can be due to a variety of reasons, such as feeling like one does not fit into any existing gender categories, or feeling like all existing gender categories are equally valid and none stand out as feeling more 'right' than the others.

9. Aravani (India)

The aravani are people from Tamil Nadu, a state in the south of India. They are people who display femininity in a masculine body, but often go through physical transformations so their bodies match their genders.

10. Ashtime (Maale, Ethiopia)

The Ashtime gender from the Maale culture of Ethiopia is a third gender that is considered to be neither male nor female. Ashtime people are seen as having special spiritual powers and as being more in tune with the natural world than other people. They often take on traditional roles such as healers, storytellers, and shamans. They were generally assigned male at birth.

11. Burrnesha (Albania)

The Burrnesha gender from Albanian culture who have taken a vow of celibacy in order to live as men. Burrneshas dress and behave like men, take on male roles such as being the head of the household, and often take a wife. They are considered to be more spiritual than other people and are seen as having special powers.

12. Bakla

Bakla are people from the Philippines who are effeminate biological men who dress and behave in ways traditionally associated with women. They are often seen as a third gender, distinct from men and women.

13. Bi-gender

Bi-gender people experience two genders, either simultaneously or at different times. These genders can be any combination of male, female, agender, etc.

14. Calabai, Calalai, and Bissu (Indonesia)

Calalai are people who are seen as being born female but take on a masculine role, while Bissu are considered to be neither male nor female. Both Calabai and Calalai may undergo surgery to remove their breasts (called 'top surgery'), while Bissu often wear both traditional masculine and feminine clothing.

15. Chuckchi Ne'uchika Shamans (Siberia)

The Chuckchi ne'uchika shamans are assigned male at birth but are believed to have been ordered by a spirit to undergo a gender transformation. They often marry males from the tribe and take on both traditionally male and female roles within the tribe.

16. Cisgender

A cisgendered person is a person who identifies with the same gender as the gender with which they were assigned at birth.

17. Cis Female

A cis female is a female who was assigned the female gender at birth and continues to identify with that gender identity.

18. Cis Male

A cis male is a male who was assigned the male gender at birth and continues to identify with that gender identity.

19. Demiboy

A demiboy is a person who identifies as partially male. They may feel that they are neither fully male nor fully female, or that they are a mix of both genders. Demiboys may or may not undergo hormone therapy or surgery to change their bodies to match their gender identity.

20. Demigender

Demigender people are those who identify as partially male or female. They may feel that they are neither fully male nor fully female, or that they are a mix of both genders.

21. Demigirl

A demigirl is a person who identifies as partially female. They may feel that they are neither fully male nor fully female, or that they are a mix of both genders. Demigirls may or may not undergo hormone therapy or surgery to change their bodies to match their gender identity.

22. Fa'afafine

Fa'afafine are a third gender in Samoan and Tongan culture. Fa'afafine are born male but identify as female and take on typically female gender roles in society. They play an important role in Samoan families and communities, and their visibility challenges traditional Western notions of gender and sexuality.

23. Fakaleiti

Fakaleiti are a third gender in traditional Polynesian societies. They are biological males who dress and behave in a feminine manner. Fakaleitis often occupy positions of respect and play an important role in Polynesian cultures, serving as healers, seers, mediators, and caretakers. In recent years, the fakaleiti identity has been adopted by many LGBTQ+ people in Polynesia as a way to express their gender and sexuality.

24. Female

The traditional or conservative definition of "female" is a person who is biologically born with ovaries and typically has the capacity to produce eggs. Increasingly, we are defining a female as a person who identifies as a woman, regardless of their biological sex. This is because we're moving toward separating the concepts of biological sex and culturally-defined genders.

25. Femme

Femme is a term used to describe a person who identifies as a woman, and/or expresses themselves in a feminine way. Femme can be used as a noun, adjective, or verb. It is often used in the LGBTQIA+ community to describe a lesbian whose comportment is traditionally feminine.

26. Femminiello (Italy)

The femminiello are a third gender from Italy. They are assigned male at birth but typically dress and behave like women. Femminiellos are often seen as lucky charms and are believed to have special powers, such as the ability to ward off evil spirits.

27. Guevedoche (Dominican Republic)

Guevedoche translates to "penis at twelve". There is an ethnic group in remote areas of the Dominican Republic who, through genetic developments, can give birth to children who are born looking like girls but grow male genetalia around age 12. This often leads to gender questioning and gender fluidity as the children age.

28. Femminiello

In southern Italy, there exists a type of male shaman-like figure called a femminiello. Femminielli are sometimes considered to be cross-dressers, androgynous, or even transgender, although most femminielli see themselves as a distinct third gender.

29. FTM

FTM is a term used to describe a person who was assigned the female gender at birth but identifies as a man. This acronym stands for 'female-to-male.'

30. Gender Apathetic

A person who is gender apathetic is someone who does not strongly lean towards identifying with one gender or another. Furthermore, they are often apathetic (or non-committal) about their attraction to one specific gender, meaning they are often bisexual.

31. Gender Fluid

A person who is gender fluid may fluctuate between genders, or they may feel like they are a mix of both genders. In one context, they may identify more strongly as male, but in another context, they may identify more as a female. It is often very much context dependant and may change over time. This is different from being bisexual because gender fluidity is about gender identity, not sexual orientation

32. Gender Neutral

A person who is gender-neutral does not identify as either a man or woman. They may have a non-binary gender identity, or they may simply not identify with any gender, and reject the dualistic thinking of the male-female binary.

33. Gender Nonconforming

A person who is gender non-conforming does not identify with the traditional gender roles assigned to their biological sex. They may

34. Gender Questioning

A person who is gender questioning is someone who is exploring and questioning their own gender identity. This may be a person who is unsure if they are transgender, or it may be a cisgender person who is curious about what it would be like to experience life as the opposite gender.

35. Gender Variant

A gender variant person is someone whose gender expression does not conform to traditional ideas about how men and women are supposed to look and behave. This could be a person who simply expresses their gender in a creative or non-traditional way.

36. Genderqueer

Genderqueer is a term that describes people with non-binary gender identities. Genderqueer people may identify as neither male nor female, or they may identify as a mix of both genders. They may also use gender-neutral pronouns such as them/they, ze/hir, or xe/xem.

37. Hermaphrodite

Hermaphrodite is an outdated and now generally disavowed term used to describe people who are intersex. Generally, this term is now strongly discouraged and often used to offend intersex people. The term intersex is now more acceptable.

38. Hijra (Kinnar)

A hijra is a person from South Asia who may be born with male genitalia but identifies as female. Hijras are sometimes considered to be a third gender, and they have a long history in many South Asian cultures such as Bangladesh, India, and Pakistan. In 2013, the government of Bangladesh officially recognise hijra as a gender.

39. Inter gender

Inter gender is a term used to describe people who have both male and female characteristics, or who fall somewhere in between the two genders. Inter gender people may identify as neither male nor female, or they may identify as a mix of both genders.

40. Intersex

The term intersex describes people who are born with genitals or other sex characteristics that do not conform to normative definitions of 'male' or 'female.' Intersex people may choose to identify as male, female, or non-binary.

41. Kathoey

A kathoey is a person from Thailand who may be born with male genitalia but identifies as female. Kathoeys are sometimes considered to be a third gender, and they have a long history in Thai culture. Since 2015 they have enjoyed enhanced legal protections in the country.

42. Lhamana (Zuni)

A lhamana is a person from the Zuni tribe in North America (primarily western New Mexico) who may be assigned male at birth but transitions to living as a female. The lhamana are considered to be a third gender in Zuni culture. Interestingly, in Zuni culture, gender roles are traditionally firmly set, but not connected to assigned sex at birth, opening space for fluid gender expression.

43. Mahu (Hawaii)

A mahu is a person from Hawaii who may be born with male genitalia but identifies as female. Mahus are also known to wear women's clothing and may take on feminine roles in their society. In ancient Hawaiian culture, mahu were revered as keepers of knowledge and skilled in the arts. Some modern scholars believe that the term "mahu" is no longer an accurate description of Native Hawaiian transgender people and prefer to use the term "wahine maoli" (Native Hawaiian woman) instead.

44. Male

The term male is a term to describe cisgendered people who were assigned male at birth and embrace that identification for themselves. A male may or may not embrace traditional masculinity roles. In today's society, there is a wide spectrum of ways to embody masculinity that can reject toxic masculinity performances of the past.

45. Maverique

A maverique is a person who defies traditional gender roles and expectations. Maveriques may identify as being of their own gender, but not male or female. Unlike other classifications, maveriqes are not genderedas they believe them to be of a distinct gender that does not fit on a spectrum of male-female. They are often creative, independent thinker, and non-conformists.

46. Metis (Nepal)

Metis are from the Nepalese culture. They are people who display femininity in a masculine body. They have been officially recognized as a third gender in Nepal since 2007.

47. MTF (Male-to-Female)

MTF is a term used to describe a person who was assigned the male gender at birth but identifies as a woman. This acronym stands for "male-to-female." A person who is MTF may choose to undergo hormone therapy and/or sex reassignment surgery to transition to living as a woman.

48. Muxe (Mexico)

The Muxe are a third gender people from the Zapotec indigenous people of Oaxaca, Mexico. Muxes are assigned male at birth but typically dress and behave in ways that are traditionally associated with women. Muxes occupy a unique and revered position in Zapotec culture, and they have been known to take on both masculine and feminine roles in their society.

49. Neither

People who identify as being of neither gender generally do not wish to be placed on a traditional gender spectrum or may identify as a third gender. 'Neither' as a gender designation is regularly used as a catch-all category on government forms for anyone who is not cisgendered.

50. Neutrois

Neutrosis was a gender identity first described in 1995. It is made up of the french terms *neutre*, meaning "neutral" *trois* meaning "three." It is used by people to explain that they are of a non-binary unidentified gender or no gender at all.

51. Ninauposkitzipxpe (Blackfoot)

The Ninauposkitzipxpe are a third gender people from the Blackfoot tribe of North America (Southern Alberta). The Ninauposkitzipxpe are assigned female at birth and typically dressed as women. However, they often took on traditionally cis-male roles within the society. The word translates to "manly-hearted woman".

52. Nadleehi and Dilbaa (Navajo)

The Navajo Native American tribe has four genders, with the two non-cis genders being Nadleehi and Dilbaa. The Nadleehi are assigned male at birth while the Dilbaa are assigned female at birth. However, both genders may take on traditionally feminine or masculine roles and dress according to their chosen gender. Nadleehi and Dilbaa genders are fluid throughout a person's life.

53. Non-binary

Non-binary is a term used to describe people who do not identify as exclusively male or female. Non-binary people may identify as being of multiple genders, no gender, or a third gender. Non-binary people may also use gender-neutral pronouns such as they/them/their.

54. Novigender

Novigender can be used to describe people who find it difficult to describe or understand how they experience gender. Novigender people may feel like their gender is ever-changing or hard to pin down.

55. Other

'Other' is a formal classification people can select on gender forms to indicate that they do not fit into a binary gender construction. It is often used on official government forms, similar to 'Neither'. People who identify as 'other' may also feel as if there is not a word to describe their experience of gender.

56. Paṇḍaka

Paṇḍakas are a gender of people who are born without the male sex organ. In ancient India, they were not considered to be men or women, but rather a third gender. They typically dress and behave like women, and many Paṇḍakas even undergo surgery to make their bodies look more female.

Paṇḍakas have a long history in India, and their role in society has changed over time. In the early Vedic period, they were seen as a separate and distinct gender, but over time they became more marginalized. By the time of the Mahabharata, they were often seen as effeminate men or as impotent men.

57. Pangender

Pangender is a term used to describe people who identify as multiple genders. Pangender people may feel like they are a combination of genders, or that their gender is constantly changing. It is often used to mean "all genders".

58. Polygender

Like pangender, polygender is a gender identity which refers to feeling multiple genders simultaneously or over time. Polygender people may feel like they are a combination of two or more genders, that their gender changes over time, or that they have no specific gender. Like many other non-binary identities, polygender is often seen as falling outside of the traditional

59. Quariwarmi (Inca, Peru)

Quariwarmi was a third gender in pre colonial Incan society. They were considered to be neither male nor female, but instead something in between. They typically dressed and behaved in ways that were considered to be more feminine than masculine. In some cases, they may have also been intersex or transgender people.

60. Sekrata (Madagascar)

The Sekrata gender is a third gender in Madagascar society. People who identify as Sekrata are generally assigned male at birth but may dress and behave in ways that are traditionally associated with women and are often respected and revered dancers.

61. Sistergirl and Brotherboy (Aboriginal Australian)

Sistergirl is a term used in Aboriginal Australian society to refer to transgender women. It is considered a respectful and positive term by those within the community.

Sistergirls are often born male but identify as female, and may undergo a traditional coming-of-age ceremony. This ceremonious event signifies their official transition into womanhood.

62. Brotherboy (Aboriginal Australia)

Brotherboys are Aboriginal Australians who are trans men. They were assigned female at birth but identify as male. They may also undergo a traditional coming-of-age rite to be recognized as males in society. Like sistergirls, brotherboys are generally respected within their own communities.

63. Third Gender

The third gender is a concept in which individuals are categorized, either by themselves or others, as neither man nor woman. It is also used to describe those who do not fit into the traditional genders of male and female. Many non-western cultures have embraced multiple genders, undermining the cultural notion that there are just two genders.

64. Tom and Dee Identities

Tom and Dee identities are those of people assigned male or female at birth, respectively, who identify as the opposite gender. For example, a person assigned male at birth who identifies as female would be considered a Tom identity. Likewise, a person assigned female at birth who identifies as male would be considered a Dee identity.

These identities are named after the Tom and Dee characters in the children's book The Gendered Society Reader. The book was written by two sociologists, Michael Kimmel and Amy Aronson, and it explores how gender impacts everyone's lives, regardless of their assigned sex.

65. Trans*

Transgender describes people whose gender identity does not match their assigned gender at birth. Often, we simply write Trans* (with an asterisk) in order to be more inclusive of all transgender people, including trans men and trans women.

66. Transmasculine

Transmasculine people are people who are AFAB (assigned female at birth) but identify as masculine (they may be a masculine woman). It is used as a term that's more specific than trans*, which could describe a wide range of gender identities.

67. Trans Man

A trans man is a person who was assigned female at birth but identifies as a man. Trans men may or may not go through surgical transitions or take medications so their body matches their gender identity.

68. Trans Woman

Trans woman people are people who are AMAB (assigned male at birth) but identify as a woman. They may or may not go through a surgical transition.

69. Transfeminine

Transfeminine people are people who are AMAB (assigned male at birth) but identify as feminine (they may be a feminine man). Note that feminine and female are not the same, where feminine is a collection of behaviors while female is a gender identification.

70. Transsexual

Transsexual is a term used to describe someone who has undergone a surgical transition to change their physical appearance to match their gender identity. This could include things like chest reconstruction (top surgery) or vaginoplasty (bottom surgery). Not all transgender people choose to have surgery, and not all who do identify as transsexual. The term is often considered outdated and offensive by many in the transgender community.

71. Transsexual Female

A transsexual female is a person who was assigned male at birth but has transitioned to live as a woman. This could include undergoing surgery and/or hormone therapy to change their physical appearance. Not all transgender women identify as transsexual, and not all transsexual women undergo surgery.

72. Transsexual Male

A transsexual male is a person who was assigned female at birth but has transitioned to live as a man. This could include undergoing surgery and/or hormone therapy to change their physical appearance. Not all transgender men identify as transsexual, and not all transsexual men undergo surgery.

73. Travesti

Travesti is a Latin American term for people who were assigned male at birth but identifu as a woman. They often live and work in all-travesti environments, such as nightclubs and brothels. They may or may not undergo hormone therapy or surgery to change their physical appearance.

74. Trigender

Trigender is a gender identity that refers to people who experience three genders: male, female, and something else that is neither of those two. This third gender can be a combination of both male and female, somewhere in between the two, or something entirely different. Trigender people may identify as any combination of genders, including but not limited to: agender, bigender, gender-fluid, or pangender. Not all trigender people experience the same three genders in the same way.

75. Two-Spirit

Two-Spirit Female is a term used to describe a Native American gender identity. Two-Spirit people are those who have both male and female spirits, and are often seen as having special powers as a result. It explains gender non-conformity in spiritual terms, seeing the person as having a spirit that spans traditional gender constructs.

76. Two-Spirit Female

Two-Spirit females are often women who identify as having both a male and female spirit. In Canada, they're often acknowledged in the acronym LGBTQI2S+. Check with the two-spirit person for the culturally appropriate way in which they define themselves.

77. Two-Spirit Male

Two-Spirit males are men who identify as having both a male and female spirit. This term (as with two-spirit female) often differs depending on the Native American culture, remembering that there were a wide range of cultures in existence before colonization. Therefore, it's important to ask the two-spirit person how they would like to be identified.

78. Waria (Indonesia)

Waria is a term used in Indonesia to describe people who are assigned male at birth but identify as women. The term itself is an Indonesian language portmanteau of woman (wanita) and man (pria). They often face discrimination within parts of conservative Indonesian culture.

79. Whakawahine (New Zealand)

Whakawahine is a Maori term used to describe people who are assigned female at birth but identify as men. It's one of the many traditional gender identities still present in Maori culture. The word translates from Whaka, meaning 'towards', and wahine, meaning 'woman'

80. Winkte (Lakota)

The Lakota people of the Sioux Native American tribe have a gender known as winkte. Winkte translates to 'two-souls person', and is used to describe someone who is assigned male at birth but has a female spirit.

81. Xanith (Oman)

The Xanith are a third gender found in Oman culture. They are assigned male at birth but undergo a social transition to live as women. This includes learning feminine gender roles and occupations typically associated with women. The Xanith are also referred to as Khanith.

It's important to recognize that our understanding of gender identity and the experiences of transgender individuals continues to evolve, and that historical examples may not perfectly align with modern concepts and terminology. Nonetheless, these examples demonstrate that diverse gender identities and expressions have existed throughout human history and across cultures.

In modern times the Transgender community has grown exponentially. Some studies suggest that approximately 0.5-1% of the population may be transgender. However, much like where history shows us that not all homosexuals want to expose themselves though fear of ridicule, not all people who identify as Transgender want to reveal themselves through fear of the same ridicule.

However, through he growth of the digital age, social media, online communities and acceptance, more and more people are beginning to feel more confident to 'come out' as trans.

There is also more representation for the trans community among celebrities such as -

1. Laverne Cox - American actress, reality television star, and LGBTQ+ advocate.
2. Chaz Bono - American writer, actor, and musician who is also the child of entertainers Sonny and Cher.
3. Jazz Jennings - American YouTube personality, author, and LGBTQ+ advocate.
4. Janet Mock - American writer, television host, and transgender rights advocate.
5. Elliot Page - Canadian actor and film-maker who rose to fame in films like "Juno" and "Inception."
6. Andreja Pejic - Australian model who has worked for designers such as Jean Paul Gaultier and Marc Jacobs.
7. Alexandra Billings - American actress who is known for her role on the television show "Transparent."
8. Jamie Clayton - American actress who starred in the Netflix series "Sense8."
9. Hari Nef - American model, actress, and writer who has appeared in campaigns for Gucci and L'Oréal Paris.
10. .Caitlyn Jenner - American television personality, retired Olympic gold medal-winning decathlete, and transgender rights advocate.

It is easy for many people to assume that many of the youth, who seemingly make up for this increase of transgendered individuals are not really trans or are 'jumping on the band wagon' While it is true that more children and adolescents are coming out as transgender or gender non-conforming in recent years, it is likely due to a combination of factors, including increased awareness and acceptance of diverse gender identities, greater access to information and resources, and reduced stigma surrounding gender diversity.

Could some Transgenderism be considered a social endemic?

An endemic is a disease or condition that is regularly found and widespread within a particular population, community or geographic area. When a particular condition, behavior, or issue is prevalent within a certain social group or community, it can also be considered a social endemic. For example in the case of bulimia, if there is a high prevalence of the disorder among a particular group of teenage girls, it may be indicative of social and cultural factors that contribute to the development of the disorder within that community. These factors could include societal pressures around body image and weight, as well as social and cultural norms around food and eating.

With regard to transgenderism, there is an argument to say that transgenderism is becoming a social endemic among younger groups, especially when schools or communities suddenly have a much higher percentage of people who identify as transgender than statistics show the national percentages to be. In other words – how is it that there ends up being high concentration of transgender identifying people in one area? When you combine this with very few of them being diagnosed with any form of gender dysmorphia, then it stands to reason that it is social, peer, environmental and cultural factors that are leading them to identify this way. When you combine this with media influence – both mainstream media and social media and factors such as the isolation and loneliness that the digital age can bring, you have all the ingredients of a social endemic.

If you look at the example of Two Spirit People from the previous list of 81 Genders, you will note that the concept of the

Two Spirit Person was constructed by Native Americans and that these people were revered for having special powers and often became Shamans. Can a blond hair, blue eyed, white skinned individual, who has no Native American heritage and has no exposure of living in that culture identify as a Two Spirit Person? Surely, they would only identify as the western white equivalent. Yet somehow there are people doing just this, which would suggest that some trans identifying people are subject to a social endemic.

If gender is truly a social construct, then surly you must be part of the society that constructed it in order to identify.

Another example that confuses people are Trans-Men who want to be or still become pregnant. Getting pregnant is a primarily female biological function. If you truly identified as a male, surly you would avoid pregnancy – which is the pinnacle of femaleness – at any cost. How does a person, with or without gender dysphoria, say that they identify as male in every way, but choose to utilise their body in a way that no male ever could.

As humans with sociable needs, we all want to belong to something and right now, being transgender - be that identifying as member of the other sex, non binary or any of the other 100 or so genders available, is one of the biggest communities to belong to.

It is key to remember that getting caught up in a social endemic is not something people consciously choose. It happens slowly over time and alters the way people see themselves or life.

On the surface, you could look at this growing trend of transgender people and say ' no harm done'. If you want to where make-up or clothes of the opposite sex then what is the harm. But as with all social endemics i.e. Bulimia, Anorexia, Cyber bullying, there is danger. The first is an increase of depression, anxiety and an increase in self harm or suicide. The second is by carrying out life altering medical procedures such as surgeries or hormone treatment.

If you regularly listen to media debates around children and transgender procedures, you will often hear the propaganda term ' Chemical Castration'.

Chemical castration is a medical treatment that involves the use of drugs to reduce the production of testosterone in the body. It is primarily used as a treatment for sexual offenders to decrease their sex drive and reduce the likelihood of reoffending. It can also be used to treat prostate cancer, as the growth of prostate cancer cells is often stimulated by testosterone.

The drugs used for chemical castration are usually administered via injection or tablets, and work by reducing the amount of testosterone produced by the testes. The most commonly used drugs for chemical castration are GnRH agonists, which work by blocking the production of luteinizing hormone (LH) and follicle-stimulating hormone (FSH), which in turn leads to a decrease in testosterone production.

This is NOT what happens to transgender children. Transgender children who have medical intervention are generally given Hormone Replacement Therapy (HRT) to induce puberty consistent with the child's gender identity, and in some cases, gender affirmation surgery.

The danger is if that a person who is transgender identifying as a result of a social endemic begin treatments only to find out they are not trans once they have left that community or the causes of the endemic have been removed the treatment cannot be reversed.

What makes a man a man

The question of what makes a man a man is complex and multifaceted, and there is no one definitive answer. Traditionally, biological sex has been the primary determinant of gender identity, with male sex assigned at birth indicating that an individual is a man. However, gender is a social construct that is shaped by cultural norms, values, and expectations, and these can vary widely across different societies and historical periods.

If you put 20, 50 or 100 men in a room and asked them what made them a man that didn't include penis bearing, you would get a different answer form each of them. Some may say someone who works hard and provides for their family and enjoys sports and beer. Some may say someone that enjoys shooting or climbing mountains or riding a motorbike.

If you take away the biology of man then many will argue that characteristics such as physical strength, aggression, and dominance are traditionally associated with masculinity and therefore make a man a man. However, these stereotypes are limiting and do not reflect the full range of human experience. In recent years, there has been a growing recognition that masculinity is not a monolithic entity, but rather a diverse and fluid concept that can be expressed in a variety of ways.

At its core, being a man is about self-identification and living authentically as one's true self. This may involve embracing traits such as emotional vulnerability, empathy, and compassion, which are often devalued in traditional definitions of masculinity. Ultimately, what makes a man a man is a deeply personal and subjective question that each individual must answer for themselves based on their own experiences, values, and beliefs.

So what makes a woman a woman?

Similar to the question of what makes a man a man, the answer to what makes a woman a woman is complex and multifaceted. Traditionally, biological sex has been the primary determinant of gender identity, with female sex assigned at birth indicating that an individual is a woman. However, gender is a social construct that is shaped by cultural norms, values, and expectations, and these can vary widely across different societies and historical periods.

Some may argue that characteristics such as nurturing, emotional sensitivity, and domesticity are traditionally associated with femininity and therefore make a woman a woman. However, these stereotypes are limiting and do not reflect the full range of human experience. In recent years, there has been a growing recognition that femininity is not a monolithic entity, but rather a diverse and fluid concept that can be expressed in a variety of ways.

At its core, being a woman is about self-identification and living authentically as one's true self. This may involve embracing traits such as assertiveness, independence, and strength, which are often devalued in traditional definitions of femininity. Ultimately, what makes a woman a woman is a deeply personal and subjective question that each individual must answer for themselves based on their own experiences, values, and beliefs. It is important to recognize that gender identity is a spectrum, and that there is no one "right" way to be a woman.

Can a Biological Male ever be a Woman

The concept of gender identity is complex, and there is ongoing debate and discussion about the relationship between biological sex and gender identity. While sex is typically assigned at birth based on genitalia and other physical characteristics, gender identity is a deeply personal and subjective experience that is shaped by a variety of factors, including biology, culture, and personal experiences.

Transgender individuals are those whose gender identity does not align with the sex assigned to them at birth. For some transgender individuals, this may involve a desire to transition to living as the gender they identify with, which may involve hormone therapy, surgery, and other medical interventions.

The area where they question gets interesting though, is experience.

Can a middle aged man, who has no experience living in the world as a woman truly identify as a woman. If our biology is independent of our gender and gender is a social construct, then how can someone who has only lived and experienced this social construct as a man identify as a woman other than a desire to have their genitalia realigned ?

After surgery how does the previous experience of life change to say 'I've really been a woman trapped in a man's body, or has the whole life experience been male and continue to be male post surgery?

If gender is a construct separate from biology, is there a potential that it all becomes a little bit of a paradox?

From a legal and social standpoint, individuals who have undergone gender transition are typically recognized as being their preferred gender. This includes recognition of their gender on official identification documents such as driver's licenses and passports, as well as protections against discrimination based on gender identity.

In short, while biological sex and gender identity are separate concepts, it is possible for a biological man to identify as a woman and live as such, and this should be respected and supported. It is important to recognize and respect the diversity of human experience, and to work towards creating a more inclusive and equitable society for all individuals, regardless of their gender identity.

Biological Advantages and Concerns

Biological advantages are traits or characteristics that confer an advantage in certain areas of life. Historically, many societies have perceived males as having certain biological advantages over females, although the extent and nature of these advantages may vary depending on the context. Here are a few examples:

1. Physical strength: On average, males tend to be physically stronger than females due to differences in muscle mass, bone density, and other factors. This advantage has historically been perceived as useful for tasks such as hunting, warfare, and physical labour.
2. Height: Males are, on average, taller than females. This can confer an advantage in certain sports or professions that require height, such as basketball or modelling.
3. Reproductive capacity: While both males and females are capable of reproducing, females bear the primary burden of pregnancy, childbirth, and lactation. This can create physical and logistical challenges for women in certain contexts, such as in the workplace or in athletic competition.

However, it is important to note that not all males possess these advantages, and not all females are disadvantaged by them. There is also a great deal of variation within each gender, and many other factors beyond biology (such as socialization, education, and access to resources) can have a significant impact on a person's opportunities and outcomes in life. It is therefore important to avoid making assumptions or generalizations based on gender, and to work towards creating a more equitable and inclusive society for all individuals.

Gender affirming surgery, also known as gender confirmation surgery or sex reassignment surgery, is a medical procedure that aims to alter the physical appearance and/or function of a person's genitalia, secondary sex characteristics, or other features to align with their gender identity. The specific effects of gender affirming surgery can vary depending on the type of surgery and the individual's goals and preferences, but here are some general considerations:

1. Hormonal changes: Many transgender individuals undergo hormone therapy prior to or in conjunction with gender affirming surgery. Hormone therapy can have a range of effects on the body, including changes to secondary sex characteristics such as body hair, breast development, and fat distribution. These changes can help a person's physical appearance to align more closely with their gender identity.

2. Physical changes to genitalia: Gender affirming surgery may involve removal of existing genitalia (as in a vaginoplasty or phalloplasty) or construction of new genitalia (as in a metoidioplasty or vaginoplasty). These surgeries can involve significant changes to the anatomy and function of the genitals, which can have both physical and psychological effects on the individual.

3. Emotional and psychological changes: For many transgender individuals, gender affirming surgery can be a deeply emotional and meaningful experience. It can help to alleviate gender dysphoria and improve overall quality of life. However, it is important to note that surgery alone

may not necessarily resolve all emotional or psychological issues related to gender identity, and ongoing support and care may be needed.

4. Risks and complications: As with any surgical procedure, gender affirming surgery carries risks of complications such as bleeding, infection, or scarring. Additionally, certain surgeries may have a higher risk of complications or may require a longer recovery period than others.

It is important to note that gender affirming surgery is just one aspect of a larger process of gender transition, and each individual's experience will be unique. Many transgender individuals find gender affirming surgery to be an important step in aligning their physical body with their gender identity, but it is not necessary or appropriate for everyone. It is important for individuals to work with qualified medical professionals to explore their options and make informed decisions about their care.

Currently, there is no definitive biological indicator or predictor that can determine if a person will be transgender. The exact causes of gender identity are not fully understood, and may involve complex interactions between genetic, hormonal, environmental, and social factors.

Some studies have suggested that there may be differences in brain structure or function between transgender and cisgender individuals, although the exact nature of these differences and their relationship to gender identity is not yet clear. Other studies have suggested that hormonal exposure during fetal development may play a role in shaping gender identity, although this is still a topic of ongoing research and debate.

It is important to note that while there may be some biological factors that contribute to gender identity, gender is ultimately a complex and multifaceted construct that is influenced by a range of social, cultural, and individual factors. Transgender individuals may have a variety of experiences and reasons for identifying with a gender that differs from the one they were assigned at birth, and these experiences and reasons are not necessarily related to any specific biological factors.

One of the main concerns of having trans people in female spaces is the potential risk to cisgender women's safety and privacy. Some people worry that allowing trans women to use women's bathrooms, locker rooms, and other gender-segregated spaces could lead to an increase in sexual assaults or harassment. It is important to remember thought that someone's gender identity does not increase their potential to be a sexual predator. We <u>ALL</u> have the potential to sexually harass or assault another, and if someone is going to act on it , they inevitably will find a way to do it.

Others argue that it is unfair to allow trans women who were assigned male at birth to compete in women's sports, as they may have an advantage due to their biology.

There are also concerns about the impact of transgender rights on women's rights, particularly in areas such as women-only spaces, female representation in politics, and protection against sex discrimination. Some feminists argue that gender identity undermines the concept of biological sex and reinforces traditional gender stereotypes, potentially harming the progress made by women's movements in challenging gender-based discrimination and oppression.

However, many transgender advocates argue that these concerns are unfounded and that trans people deserve equal access to public spaces and protections under the law. They argue that trans women are not a threat to cisgender women's safety and that allowing them to use women's spaces is a matter of human rights and dignity. Additionally, they argue that transgender rights are not in opposition to women's rights, but rather are an important part of the broader struggle for gender equality and social justice – which is the same place trans woman where in when they were welcomed in to the fight back in the 1980's

Transgender people have always existed, but it is only in recent years that society has begun to understand and acknowledge their experiences. Despite this progress, there is still much work to be done to ensure that transgender individuals are treated with dignity, respect, and equality.

First and foremost, transgender people should be treated as the gender with which they identify. This means using their chosen name and pronouns, and respecting their gender expression. It is important to understand that gender identity is not a choice, and that transgender individuals should not have to justify or prove their gender to others.

In addition to respecting gender identity, it is crucial to support transgender individuals in accessing healthcare, including gender-affirming medical treatments such as hormone therapy and surgeries. These treatments are often essential for transgender individuals to feel comfortable and authentic in their bodies, and should be available without discrimination or barriers.

Transgender individuals also face significant discrimination in employment, housing, education, and other areas of life. It is important to advocate for policies and laws that protect transgender individuals from discrimination and harassment, and to hold accountable those who perpetrate violence or discrimination against transgender people.

Beyond these basic rights, transgender individuals also deserve to have their experiences and perspectives represented in all aspects of society. This means including transgender voices in media, entertainment, and politics, and working to dismantle the systemic barriers that have excluded transgender individuals from positions of power and influence.

Finally, it is important to recognize that the experiences of transgender individuals are diverse and intersectional, and that different individuals may have different needs and priorities. Transgender people may also experience discrimination and marginalization based on other aspects of their identity, such as race, ethnicity, disability, or socioeconomic status. It is therefore essential to center the voices and experiences of transgender individuals themselves, and to work towards a more just and equitable world for all.

In conclusion, the 21st century should be a time of progress and liberation for transgender individuals. By treating transgender people with respect and dignity, supporting their access to healthcare and other basic rights, and centering their experiences and perspectives, we can create a more inclusive and just society for all. It is up to all of us to do our part to make this vision a reality.

Don't miss out!

Visit the website below and you can sign up to receive emails whenever Amanda Walker publishes a new book. There's no charge and no obligation.

https://books2read.com/r/B-A-XDVX-WPYIC

BOOKS 2 READ

Connecting independent readers to independent writers.